AMBULANCE RESCUE

EMERGENCY VEHICLES

Deborah Chancellor

W

FRANKLIN WATTS

LONDON • SYDNEY

First published in 2012 by Franklin Watts
338 Euston Road, London NW1 3BH

Franklin Watts Australia
Level 17/207 Kent Street, Sydney, NSW 2000

A CIP catalogue record for this book
is available from the British Library
Dewey Classification: 629.2'2234
ISBN: 978 1 4451 0873 5

Printed in China

Series editor: Adrian Cole/Amy Stephenson
Editor: Sarah Ridley
Art direction: Peter Scoulding
Designer: Steve Prosser
Picture researcher: Diana Morris

Franklin Watts is a division of
Hachette Children's Books,
an Hachette UK company.
www.hachette.co.uk

Picture credits:
Avico Ltd/Alamy: 15t.
Stuart Clarke/Rex Features: 19t.
Ashley Cooper/Alamy: 12-13, 13t.
Ian Danbury/Dreamstime: 18-19.
Gary Dobner/Alamy: 11.
Fire Photo/Alamy: 9t.
A Wesley Floyd/Shutterstock: 5t.
Image Source/Rex Features: 6.
Timothy Large/Dreamstime: 8-9.
Dennis MacDonald/Alamy: 4.
Travis Manley/istockphoto: front cover, 5b.
Roberto Marinello/Dreamstime: 7.
Bruce Miller/Alamy: 16.
one-image photography/Alamy: 10.
Realimage/Alamy: 14-15.
Royal Flying Doctor Service: 17.
Tupungato/Shutterstock: 21t.
Zmiel Photography/istockphoto: 20-21.

Every attempt has been made to clear copyright.
Should there be any inadvertent omission,
please apply to the publisher for rectification.

Contents

Flashing lights

Ambulances carry sick or injured people to hospital. This ambulance is speeding to an emergency. Lights flash and **sirens** wail.

WHOOEE!

The 'star of life' **symbol** appears on many ambulances around the world. It shows that they belong to the emergency medical services.

Flashing lights

AMBULANCE

Emergency care

The ambulance crew are called **paramedics**. They use a **stretcher** to put a patient into the ambulance.

Paramedics are trained to do emergency first aid. They can use all the life-saving **equipment** on board the ambulance.

Blood pressure equipment

Equipment for broken limbs

Patient seat belt

Stretcher

Breathing equipment

Rapid reaction

A fast paramedic car rushes to an accident. The paramedics use the **two-way radio** to call for more ambulances if they are needed.

WHOOOEEEE!

The front of the car has the word 'AMBULANCE' written on it backwards. Drivers read the word in their driving mirrors and then know to move out of the way.

VROOOOOOM!

Traffic buster

A speedy paramedic motorbike zips through crowded streets to reach an emergency. **Panniers** on the motorbike carry life-saving equipment.

The motorbike helmet is fitted with a two-way radio.

BEEEEP! BEEEEP!

LONDON AMBULANCE SERVICE

NHS

The bright colours and flashing lights on a paramedic motorbike make it easy to spot on the road.

Rough ride

Sturdy off-road ambulances are built to drive over rough ground. The tyres have a heavy **tread** to stop the ambulance from skidding.

BBRRRR!

AMBULANCE

JLANCE nk E. Mellor

Frank E. Mellor

A searchlight on the ambulance's **bonnet** helps to find injured people at night.

RRR!

Airlift

A helicopter that flies sick people to hospital is called an air ambulance. Important medical equipment is kept on board.

An air ambulance can fly to places that cannot be reached any other way.

CHUPPPA!

WHUPPPA!

G-SASA

Bond

SERVICE

AMBULANCE

Flying doctor

Some people who live far from towns and cities need planes to bring doctors and nurses to them.

VROOOOOOMM!

EEOOOOOWW!

Propeller

This patient needs to be flown to a hospital far away. The plane's crew of doctors and nurses will care for him during the long flight.

Royal Flying Doctor

TP 30

An army ambulance is covered with strong metal **plates** to protect it from bullets, **mines** and explosions.

CHUPPPA!

WHUPPPA!

WHUPPPA!

CHUPPPA!

63

The **Red Cross** symbol tells the enemy that this is an ambulance.

Armies use air ambulances to fly injured soldiers out of **war zones**.

19

Colourful speed boats are used as ambulances in places where water is the only or the quickest way to travel.

WHOOEE!

AZIENDA ULSS

AMBULANZA

SPLASH!

A siren warns other boats to move out of the way. The boat carries medical equipment and trained staff to care for patients.

BRUUMMM!

EZIANA

KODEN

6V 23573

AMBULANZA

Glossary

blood pressure the force of blood pushing on the sides of the tubes that carry blood around your body

bonnet the cover over a vehicle's engine

emergency a sudden or dangerous event or situation

equipment the things you need to do something

mines bombs hidden under the ground

panniers boxes or bags on the back of a bike

paramedics people who are trained to do emergency first aid

plates protective metal armour

propeller spinning blades that drive a boat or plane forward

Red Cross an organisation that protects people in danger

sirens a loud hooting or wailing sound

stretcher a bed with handles for carrying sick or injured people

symbol a picture or thing that stands for something else

tread the patterns on a rubber tyre

two-way radio a radio set you use to talk to somebody far away

war zones dangerous places where battles are fought

Quiz

1. Why is the word 'AMBULANCE' often written backwards on an ambulance?

2. What are paramedics?

3. Why do ambulances display the 'star of life' symbol?

4. What is kept in the panniers on a paramedic motorbike?

5. What is an air ambulance?

6. How are army ambulances protected from attack?

Answers:

1. The word 'AMBULANCE' is written backwards so other drivers can read it in their mirrors. This tells them to move out of the way.

2. Paramedics are people who are trained to do emergency first aid.

3. The 'star of life' symbol on an ambulance shows it is an emergency medical vehicle.

4. The panniers on a paramedic motorbike contain life-saving equipment.

5. An air ambulance is a helicopter that flies sick or injured people to hospital.

6. Army ambulances are covered with strong metal plates to protect them from attack.

Index

WHOOEE!